Evaluation Report Wastewater Management Controlling and Abating Combined Sewer Overflows

U.S. Environmental Protection Agency

The BiblioGov Project is an effort to expand awareness of the public documents and records of the U.S. Government via print publications. In broadening the public understanding of government and its work, an enlightened democracy can grow and prosper. Ranging from historic Congressional Bills to the most recent Budget of the United States Government, the BiblioGov Project spans a wealth of government information. These works are now made available through an environmentally friendly, print-on-demand basis, using only what is necessary to meet the required demands of an interested public. We invite you to learn of the records of the U.S. Government, heightening the knowledge and debate that can lead from such publications.

Included are the following Collections:

Budget of The United States Government
Presidential Documents
United States Code
Education Reports from ERIC
GAO Reports
History of Bills
House Rules and Manual
Public and Private Laws

Code of Federal Regulations
Congressional Documents
Economic Indicators
Federal Register
Government Manuals
House Journal
Privacy act Issuances
Statutes at Large

Office of Inspector General

Evaluation Report

Wastewater Management

Controlling and Abating Combined Sewer Overflows

Report No. 2002-P-00012   August 26, 2002

Inspector General Resource Center Conducting the Audit:	Eastern Audit and Evaluation Resource Center Boston, Massachusetts Office New York, New York Office
Regions Covered:	Regions 1, 3, and 5
Program Office Involved:	Office of Wastewater Management
Report Contributors:	Ira Brass, Project Manager Robert Hairston Linda Fuller Harry Silver Edward Baldinger John Coll, General Engineer

Abbreviations

CSO:	Combined Sewer Overflow
EPA:	Environmental Protection Agency
NPDES:	National Pollutant Discharge Elimination System
OIG:	Office of Inspector General

Cover Photo: An outfall in the Boston, Massachusetts area (photo by EPA OIG)

UNITED STATES ENVIRONMENTAL PROTECTION AGENCY
WASHINGTON, DC 20460

OFFICE OF
INSPECTOR GENERAL

August 26, 2002

MEMORANDUM

SUBJECT: Report Number: 2002-P-00012
           Controlling and Abating Combined Sewer Overflows

FROM: Dan Engelberg /s/
           Director for Program Evaluation, Water Programs

TO: G. Tracy Mehan
           Assistant Administrator for Water

Attached is our report, *Controlling and Abating Combined Sewer Overflows*. This report contains issues and recommendations that affect EPA, state, and local water programs.

This report contains findings that describe problems the Office of Inspector General (OIG) has identified and corrective actions the OIG recommends. The audit report represents the opinion of the OIG and the findings contained in this report do not necessarily represent the final EPA position. Final determinations on matters of this report will be made by EPA managers in accordance with established EPA audit resolution procedures.

In accordance with EPA Order 2750, you as the Action Official are required to provide this office a written response to the report within 90 days. Your response should address all recommendations, and include milestone dates for corrective actions planned but not completed.

We have no objection to the release of this report to the public.

Should you or your staff have any questions about this report, please contact me at (202) 566-0830 or Ira Brass at (212) 637-3057.

Executive Summary

Combined Sewer Overflows (CSOs) are the total discharges into water bodies of untreated domestic, commercial, and industrial waste and wastewater, as well as storm water runoff, from a Combined Sewer System. Such a system collects and transports both sanitary sewage and storm water runoff in a single-pipe system to a wastewater treatment facility. Overflows can impair water quality and adversely affect the health of humans, animals, and aquatic organisms, as well as cause beach closings and fishing and recreational restrictions.

The Environmental Protection Agency (EPA) issued a CSO Policy in 1994, and states and communities have implemented CSO programs with varying success. Since 1978, the number of CSO permittees has been reduced from approximately 1,300 to 859. Some states have given the CSO program a higher priority than others. To evaluate this issue on a national level, we sought to determine:

- What barriers, if any, need to be overcome in implementing the CSO Policy?

- What are examples of better CSO practices?

- What levels of water quality or other outcomes are used to measure CSO Policy accomplishments? What improvements in the level of water quality have been achieved?

Significant Barriers Remain

An estimated $44.7 billion is needed nationwide for CSO abatement efforts, and raising sufficient funding for often expensive projects is obviously a significant barrier for many communities. The Clean Water State Revolving Fund is a major funding mechanism, but even its vast resources cannot meet the demand. Another key barrier that we noted is finding suitable sites for needed facilities.

Many Promising Practices Noted

A key part of our review was to identify promising practices already implemented by some of the CSO communities. Despite the barriers noted, states and communities demonstrated numerous promising practices that could be employed in the CSO programs of others to improve operations, reduce costs, and eliminate some of the aforementioned barriers. These promising practices included a variety of technical approaches and innovations, state grant programs, government cooperative efforts, public education initiatives, and neighborhood improvements. Numerous examples of these best practices are in Chapter 4 of this report. However, there is a need for a central mechanism within EPA to disseminate this information.

Limited Data Available on Water Quality Improvements

We found that many communities do not as yet have the data to determine the effect of CSO controls on water quality. Most communities were only monitoring the number, volume, and duration of CSO discharges, and did not have data on the effect CSO controls were having on the quality of receiving waters. This was because EPA does not require monitoring until completion of CSO projects. Consequently, it could not be determined until it was too late whether each CSO project being undertaken was a wise investment of taxpayers' dollars.

Watershed Approach Should Be Considered

Because of the broad variety of pollution sources affecting water bodies, a watershed management approach is needed to adequately address water quality. While CSO discharges are a significant pollution source, eliminating them will not always ensure that water quality standards will be met. Sanitary sewer overflows, storm water, pollution from upstream sources, and concentrated animal feeding operations can also impair water bodies. Attainment of clean water can only be accomplished through a concerted effort to limit *all* sources of pollutants.

Recommendations

Our recommendations to the Assistant Administrator for Water to improve the CSO program include developing a system to disseminate lessons learned and better practices about CSOs. Also, EPA should work with CSO permitting authorities and communities to assure the performance of interim reviews regarding water quality, and take a leadership role in encouraging the use of watershed approaches and having states and communities work together to accomplish clean water.

Agency Response

In his July 15, 2002 response to our draft report (Appendix 1), the Assistant Administrator for Water agreed with all but one of the findings and recommendations. He disagreed with our recommendation from Chapter 5 that EPA amend the CSO Policy to require communities to perform interim reviews of the water quality impacts of CSO upgrade projects. Although he agreed with our contention that these reviews are often beneficial, he argued that it would be more expedient if EPA achieved this by working with individual communities and permitting authorities rather than through a policy change. We have changed this recommendation, but will monitor EPA's success in achieving this objective.

Table of Contents

Executive Summary .... *i*

Chapters

1	Introduction	1
	Purpose	*1*
	Background	*1*
	Scope and Methodology	*4*
2	CSO Implementation Efforts Have Varied	7
3	Significant Barriers Remain	11
4	Many Promising Practices Used by States and Communities Have Improved CSO Program	19
5	Limited Data Available on Improvements to Water Quality	27
6	CSO Efforts Need to Focus More on Entire Watershed	31

Exhibits

1	Nine Minimum Controls and Long-Term Control Plans	39
2	Review Participants	41

Appendices

1	Agency Response	43
2	Distribution	51

Report No. 2002-P-00012

Chapter 1
Introduction

Purpose

The cost to make improvements to abate Combined Sewer Overflows (CSOs) is estimated by an Environmental Protection Agency (EPA) Needs Survey at $44.7 billion. CSOs are the largest category of our Nation's wastewater infrastructure that still need to be addressed. They impact 40 million Americans in 32 states (including the District of Columbia) through impaired water quality that adversely affects the health of humans, animals, and aquatic organisms, and cause beach closings and fishing and recreational restrictions.

EPA issued a CSO Policy in 1994 that became law in December 2000. While EPA has instituted the program, there is uncertainty about what actions have been taken and their effectiveness. An earlier Office of Inspector General report focusing on EPA Region 2 noted various levels of success regarding CSO actions. To evaluate this issue on a national level, our objectives were to determine:

- What barriers, if any, need to be overcome in implementing the CSO Policy?

- What are examples of better practices?

- What levels of water quality or other outcomes are used to measure CSO Policy accomplishments? What improvements in the level of water quality have been achieved?

Background

CSOs are the total discharges of untreated domestic, commercial, and industrial waste and wastewater, as well as storm water runoff, from a Combined Sewer System. Such a system collects and transports both sanitary sewage and storm water runoff in a single-pipe system to a wastewater treatment facility. As shown in Figure 1.1, a CSO event occurs when the total wastewater and storm water flow exceeds the capacity of the Combined Sewer System and, by design, discharges directly to the receiving water body. This usually occurs after excessive precipitation.

Suspended solids, toxins, nutrients, heavy metals, pathogens, floatable matter, oils, and oxygen-demanding compounds are among the pollutants discharged with a CSO. Historically, CSOs have received very little, if any, treatment. Because of the flow volumes and the nature of the pollutants discharged, CSOs may pose a significant public health and pollution threat. Pollutants in CSO discharges have been shown to be a major contributor to non-attainment of water quality standards. Non-attainment events may degrade the physical characteristics of surface waters, threaten potential drinking water supplies, and impair the established uses of receiving waters (such as through beach closures and shellfish harvesting restrictions).

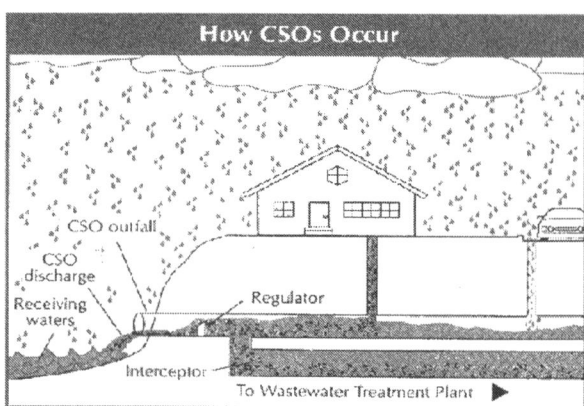

Figure 1.1: How CSOs Occur

EPA estimates the total number of Combined Sewer Systems represents 859 National Pollutant Discharge Elimination System (NPDES) permittees, regulating 9,471 CSO discharge points, located primarily in the Northeast, Middle Atlantic, Midwest, and Northwest. The map in Figure 1.2 shows the location of CSO communities. Combined Sewer Systems were constructed prior to the 1950s and exist primarily in older, urban communities. They vary dramatically in size, number of outfalls, and frequency and volume of discharge. About 90 percent of the Systems are found in communities of fewer than 100,000 people, and about 60 percent serve communities with fewer than 10,000 people.

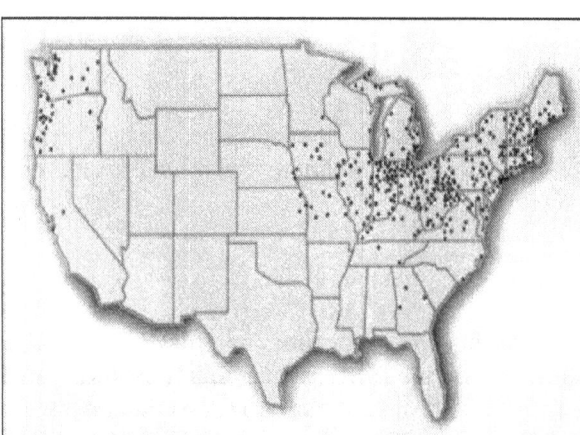

Figure 1.2: CSO Communities in the United States

National projections of annual CSO discharges are estimated at 1,260 billion gallons per year. CSOs discharge into the following receiving waters: rivers (43 percent); streams (38 percent); oceans, estuaries, and bays (5 percent); lakes and ponds (2 percent); and other waters (ditches, canals, etc.) (12 percent).

In EPA's 1996 Needs Survey for all wastewater needs (the latest available), the $44.7 billion listed for CSO capital improvements (out of a total $120.6 billion) was the largest category of wastewater infrastructure facilities. As required by the Clean Water Act, states and EPA jointly prepare a survey of total documented and modeled needs by state for publicly owned wastewater treatment facilities. The Needs Survey represents the capital investment necessary to build publicly owned wastewater treatment facilities and other types of facilities eligible for State Revolving Funds. These other facilities include storm water, combined sewers, and nonpoint source replacement and rehabilitation. The $44.7 billion amount has remained constant, according to a 1999 House of Representatives Subcommittee Hearing on Clean Water Infrastructure and Wet Weather Flows Legislation.

CSO Policy

On September 8, 1989, EPA published a National CSO Strategy recommending that all CSOs be identified and categorized according to status of compliance with NPDES requirements. In order to accelerate efforts to bring CSOs into compliance with the Clean Water Act, EPA met with state and local officials as well as environmental groups in early 1992. The result was the development of EPA's CSO Policy published on April 11, 1994, which is currently in use. The Policy provides guidance to permittees with CSOs, NPDES authorities, and state water quality standards authorities for coordinating the planning, selection, and implementation of CSO controls that meet Clean Water Act requirements.

In December 2000, Congress passed the Wet Weather Combined Sewer/Sanitary Sewer/Watershed Pilot Project Program as part of EPA's fiscal 2001 funding bill. With the signing of this bill, the CSO Policy became a statutory part of the Clean Water Act. The law required EPA to (1) prepare and issue documents that provide guidance; (2) report to Congress on progress made; and (3) provide Congress with a report summarizing environmental impacts, resources spent, and technologies used. EPA accomplished the first task by issuing its July 31, 2001, *Guidance: Coordinating CSO Long-Term Planning with Water Quality Standards Reviews*. The second task was accomplished in December 2001 when EPA issued *Implementation and Enforcement of the Combined Sewer Overflow Control Policy*. The third task is to be accomplished by issuing a report to Congress in 2003.

On May 31, 1995, EPA issued its *Guidance for Nine Minimum Controls*. These controls can reduce CSOs and their effects on water quality. They do not require major engineering studies and usually can be implemented in less than 2 years. According to the 1994 CSO Policy, CSO permittees are responsible for developing and implementing long-term control plans that will ultimately result in compliance with Clean Water Act requirements. Details are in Exhibit 1.

CSO Control Measures

Communities use three types of CSO controls to implement the CSO Policy:

- *Collection system controls* are measures that remove flow from, or divert flow within, the Combined Sewer System to maximize the conveyance of flow through the system to the treatment facility. This category includes infiltration/inflow control, pump station capacity upgrades, expanded interceptor capacity, regulating devices and backwater gates, inflatable dams, flow diversion, real-time control, and sewer separation.

- *Storage controls* are measures that temporarily store combined sewage for subsequent treatment at the treatment facility once capacity becomes available. This category includes in-line storage, retention basins, and tunnels.

- *Treatment controls* are measures that reduce the pollutant load in CSO discharges. This category includes coarse screening, primary sedimentation, increased treatment plant capacity, swirl/vortex technologies, and disinfection.

EPA's CSO Progress Report

In its December 2001 progress report, EPA found that cities that had made substantial progress and investments in CSO control were realizing public health and water quality benefits. EPA identified various challenges, including financial, water quality standard reviews, and information management and performance measurement. These same issues were noted by our review and are addressed in subsequent chapters of this report.

Scope and Methodology

Our ability to draw valid conclusions concerning barriers and promising practices is based on applying an evaluation design involving collecting information from a broad range of sources. To determine the ways that CSO policy is arrived at and implemented in communities, and the relationships among levels of government in different parts of the country, we reviewed documents and conducted interviews and site visits at four different administrative levels. A complete listing of all participants visited and interviewed is in Exhibit 2; a summary follows.

- We conducted interviews at EPA's Office of Wastewater Management, which sets and administers national policy and guidance on CSOs. This office is within the EPA Office of Water.

- We interviewed staff in EPA's Great Lakes National Program Office and 3 of EPA's 10 regional offices: Regions 1, 3, and 5. EPA's regional offices work in partnership with the states and monitor their implementation of the CSO Policy. These three regions contain 678 of the 859 CSO permittees identified by EPA nationally, or 79 percent.

- We conducted structured interviews of officials in the state environmental protection offices of eight states within the three regions reviewed – Connecticut, Illinois, Indiana, Massachusetts, Michigan, Ohio, Pennsylvania, and Vermont. We conducted these interviews to determine their management of CSOs in the communities. We also reviewed and analyzed water quality reports and CSO policies, procedures, guidance, permits, correspondence, manuals, status reports, needs surveys, and state revolving fund information. These states contain a large majority of the communities with CSOs in the three EPA regions (549 of the 859 CSO permittees identified by EPA nationally, or 64 percent).

- Most of our data collected was from extensive site visits in 22 communities with CSOs. In several instances our site visits involved regional groupings of communities. We administered structured interviews designed to solicit the thoughts of various officials in each of these communities. As part of each visit, we toured facilities and in some cases reviewed water quality and status reports. For each site, our team included a degreed engineer with extensive experience in wastewater collection systems. We selected the communities based on our review of information provided by EPA and state officials. Although we do not claim that these communities are "statistically representative" of CSO communities overall, we believe that because they encompass a variety of conditions (size, type of receiving water, and CSO approach), findings based on them will be useful in identifying barriers and promising approaches that can be used elsewhere.

To include a broader range of opinions, we interviewed representatives from two industry organizations that represent municipal sewage treatment officials: the CSO Partnership and the Association of Metropolitan Sewerage Agencies. We also held large scale "roundtable discussions" in three states (Michigan, Ohio, and Pennsylvania) that included representatives of other communities, outside consultants, and a court monitor responsible for oversight of CSO contols in the Rouge River Watershed.

We conducted field work from April through November 2001. We conducted this evaluation in accordance with *Government Auditing Standards* issued by the Comptroller General of the United States.

Prior Audit Coverage

We previously issued a report on the CSO program, *Combined Sewer Overflows in Region 2* (2001-P-00001), dated January 3, 2001. The report noted that despite steady water quality improvement over the past two decades, CSOs continued to impair New York and New Jersey water bodies. In that report, we also found that certain communities had made significant efforts to address CSOs, resulting in varying degrees of success.

Chapter 2
CSO Implementation Efforts Have Varied

States have been implementing CSO programs for decades with varying success. Some states have given the CSO program a high priority, which resulted in the reduction of CSO permittees/outfalls. Other states have not given implementing CSO projects as much priority. In addition, states were at different stages in reviewing and approving long-term control plans for implementing CSO projects. Two states in our review offered financial assistance to communities through state grant funding accompanied with low interest loans.

Differing Progress in Eliminating CSOs

We found that the overall progress made on CSO abatement appeared to be consistent with the level of priority a state gave to the CSO program. The situation in three states illustrates this point.

- The Vermont Department of Environmental Conservation was a leader in ensuring that most of its communities had undergone sewer separation during the 1990s. CSO permittees were reduced from 27 in 1990 to 7 in 2001. CSO projects received priority ranking for State Revolving Fund loans and were eligible for 25-percent state grant funding. (Further details on grant programs are in Chapter 4.)

- A Connecticut Department of Environmental Protection memorandum, issued February 22, 2001, stated that CSOs were a priority water quality issue for years, as evidenced by pollution abatement orders that had been issued as early as 1975. CSO projects received priority ranking for State Revolving Fund loans and were eligible for 50-percent state grant funding. While there were 13 CSO communities with 246 outfalls during the 1970s and 1980s, there were only 8 CSO communities with 121 outfalls in 2000.

- Pennsylvania, which has the greatest number of CSO communities (155) and discharge points (1,662) in the nation, has actually had its CSO numbers increase slightly (due generally to newly discovered discharges). CSO abatement was not a high priority, according to the Pennsylvania Department of Environmental Protection officials, who said they had not been proactive during the first round of CSO permits. Competing priorities for staff included in-stream assessments, combined animal feeding operations, and total maximum daily loads. The state included conditions for the implementation of the CSO policy in its NPDES permits. However, compliance was low and the state did not follow up because of limited resources and competing priorities. Since December 2000, Region 3 pressured Pennsylvania to give CSOs a higher priority. Pennsylvania issued a CSO policy on January 30, 2002, committing significant state time and resources. Additionally, the General Assembly of Pennsylvania introduced a bill to establish a grant program to assist municipalities in addressing CSO impacts.

EPA regional staff also indicated that prior to the passage of the 2000 Wet Weather Water Quality Act, some states saw the CSO Policy as a policy and not as a law or regulation. This prior viewpoint had an impact on the level of CSO policy implementation.

Varying Levels of Long-Term Control Plan Implementation

We also found states with varying levels of success in developing and implementing long-term control plans for CSO. For example, we noted the following for four different states we visited in Region 5.

- **Indiana:** Only 6 communities (less than 10 percent of the 88 CSO communities) had submitted their plans for approval. The Indiana Department of Environmental Management had scheduled dates for additional submissions through 2003.

- **Michigan:** All plans had been submitted and received some degree of state approval.

- **Ohio:** Only 29 of 91 CSO communities submitted plans, 12 of which have been approved.

- **Illinois:** Most communities were meeting state treatment standards for CSOs. Where CSOs continue to cause or contribute to water quality standards violations, additional long-term controls will be needed.

EPA's 2001 Report to Congress noted that municipal progress was slow in developing long-term control plans. Specifically, the report indicated that only 34 percent of CSO communities reviewed had submitted draft plans for approval.

Once long-term control plans are approved, communities are taking different approaches in controlling CSOs (such as separating sewers, constructing retention basins, and building storage tunnels). Also, some states implement one project to control several CSO outfalls in neighboring communities. This maximizes cost savings while eliminating multiple CSOs within one geographical area. For example, since 1994, the Metropolitan Water Reclamation District of Greater Chicago received $151 million for a tunnel and reservoir project covering 40 CSO communities.

Strategies and Guidance

All states visited have either developed CSO strategies and programs to abate CSOs or adopted the policy to their existing program. Additionally, some states adopted criteria to further assist with implementing their programs. For example, in July 2000, Indiana passed Senate Enrolled Act 431 to provide relief and facilitate long-term control plans for communities with substantial and widespread economic and social hardship. In addition, several states had CSO requirements that predated the 1994 policy. For example:

- Illinois had a CSO policy since the 1960s. Several communities addressed and planned for CSO needs in the mid-1980s through Municipal Compliance Plans. Most sewer separation projects were completed even before the CSO Policy was written.

- In Ohio, Toledo completed construction of an underground storage tunnel in 1993 that had been initiated in 1987. This project eliminated 12 of Toledo's 35 CSO points.

- Michigan adopted a CSO strategy in January 1990 to establish enforceable deadlines for CSO controls and to eliminate or adequately treat all CSOs.

Most states have adopted EPA's approaches for targeting CSO controls and discharge requirements. States may adopt requirements that are even more stringent than EPA's CSO Policy. For example, EPA's CSO Policy's presumption approach allows an average of four untreated CSO events per year, while Michigan adopted a more stringent requirement that does not allow for any untreated discharges.

Conclusion

States and communities have been working for decades addressing CSOs. States in all three regions we visited made efforts to abate CSOs, but not all states set CSO abatement as a high priority, which ultimately delayed progress towards eliminating CSO outfalls. Other competing priorities included stormwater, in stream assessments, combined animal feeding operations, and total maximum daily loads. While all states adopted CSO strategies and guidelines, long-term control plan implementations were at different stages.

Chapter 3
Significant Barriers Remain

The nation has made steady progress reducing the number of CSOs. The number of systems with CSOs has been reduced from approximately 1,300 to 859 since 1978, based on data provided by EPA. We visited and interviewed officials from 21 communities and 1 water authority (comprising 43 communities). At each one, we asked officials about the barriers they encountered in addressing CSOs. They provided us with numerous items, including: the expensiveness of projects, the lack of available funding, competing priorities, increasing user rates, decreasing industrial bases, the absence of grant programs, state legal requirements, land availability, community opposition, water quality issues, and other pollution sources.

We analyzed these many concerns and combined them into two significant barriers that hampered efforts to achieve EPA's goal of ensuring that there is a comprehensive and coordinated effort to achieve cost effective CSO controls that ultimately meet appropriate health and environmental objectives:

- Raising and obtaining sufficient funding for often expensive projects.

- Finding suitable sites for the needed facilities.

While progress is being made in addressing the barriers, the task can at times be daunting. Table 3.1 shows how the majority of these communities encountered these barriers. The table includes six communities that encountered both.

Barriers	Number
Funding Limitations	15
Finding Suitable Sites	8

Table 3.1: Major Barriers

In Chapter 4, we will describe some of the promising practices states and communities have developed or implemented to address these barriers. The water quality barriers are further discussed in Chapter 6.

Funding Most Significant Barrier

As can be seen from Table 3.1, funding was cited most often as a major barrier to implementation of EPA's CSO Control Policy (15 of the 22 visited). This is not surprising considering the huge sums that are often necessary to implement long-term control plans. EPA's 1996 Needs Survey (the latest available) lists CSO capital improvements at $44.7 billion. Communities large and small, suburbs and inner cities, often cited funding as critical. Although EPA and individual states have devised approaches to facilitate many projects, the bulk of resources are raised locally. Significant variations exist among different types of communities in their ability to raise the funds needed.

Communities Face Affordability Issues

The expense of controlling and abating CSOs can strain the financial resources of any community. Even obtaining a State Revolving Fund loan (to be discussed further in the next subsection) by itself can create significant debt repayment pressure on a locality's budget. Examples of the funding impact on small, mid-sized, and large communities follow:

- **Small Community:** Paulding, Ohio, a village with a population of approximately 3,000, had a CSO need of $11.7 million, according to the 1996 Needs Survey. Paulding had to struggle to finance its CSO projects with bonds and notes because it could not get State Revolving Funds. It increased sewer utility rates and initiated a city income tax. While it has eliminated 16 of its 18 CSO points over the past 10 years, its proposed long-term control plan foresees a separation project that will take another 20 years to complete.

- **Mid-Sized Community:** New Haven, Connecticut, a city with a population of about 100,000, had an estimated CSO need of $291 million, according to its 1988 Facilities Plan. New Haven has been working toward the removal of CSOs since 1981, and has reduced its number of CSOs from 22 to 19. The City has borrowed $28 million from the State Revolving Fund and also received $13 million in grants from the State of Connecticut. Nonetheless, New Haven Water Pollution Control Authority officials estimated its current user rates will rise from $165 to $630 per annum to pay for all the CSO work.

- **Large Community:** Detroit, Michigan, has a mixed sewer system serving about 3 million people (about 1 million in the city and 2 million in 77 neighboring communities). The City's Preferred Plan estimated a need for about $1 billion in CSO work. The Detroit Water and Sewerage Department has 78 CSO outfalls that discharge approximately 20 billion gallons each year. Several projects have already been initiated. Detroit has received about $188 million in State Revolving Fund loans and $98 million in grant funds for CSO projects. In funding the work, a major issue has been how much is to be funded by the City of Detroit versus the suburban communities that it services.

One issue facing all communities is the competing priorities that exist for the limited financial resources. Many local officials told us they have other important projects requiring substantial financing, such as highway and road repair, wastewater treatment plants, park maintenance, libraries, and hospitals. In addition, they have more visible services to fund, such as police, fire, and emergency services; education; and sanitation. For example, the mayor of Haverhill, Massachusetts, wrote to EPA that its ability to borrow for CSO work was being impeded by financial difficulties stemming in part from a $1-million-a-month operating loss at the city's hospital.

The Association of Metropolitan Sewerage Agencies, in a February 2002 report, *The National Response to Combined Sewer Overflows*, noted that annual investments in CSO long-term control plan implementation represented an unusually large portion of a community's total capital improvement plan budget. According to its survey respondents, communities had dedicated, on average, 36.8 percent of their capital improvement plan budgets for CSO controls. Further, EPA, in its December 2001 report to Congress, noted that addressing competing priorities was a concern.

State requirements can also limit a community's options. For example, the Headlee Amendment to Michigan's State Constitution (passed in 1978) and "Proposal A" (passed in 1994) limit the ability of local governments to fund projects such as sewage infrastructure through property taxes. Communities cannot increase rates to pay for CSO and Sanitary Sewer Overflow improvements through water rates; they need to submit increases to residents through tax increases.

Communities that are already economically distressed will have difficulty funding CSO projects. The loss of business or weakening of the industrial base of a community can also be a contributing factor to affordability. For example, the Environmental Law Institute reported in its 1999 report, *Plumbing the Future, Sewage Infrastructure and Sustainability in Western Pennsylvania,* that the area was facing an estimated $3 billion to address CSOs while the area's population was significantly declining and the tax base shrinking. We also noted that many municipalities in Region 5 have lost tax revenues because of a declining industrial base.

State Revolving Funding Limited

The Clean Water State Revolving Fund program is one of the major funding mechanisms for CSO communities, but even with its significant resources it cannot provide all the money needed to address the CSO problem. Further, there are other competing water project needs for State Revolving Funds besides CSOs, such as secondary and advanced treatment, new interceptor and collector sewers, infiltration/inflow correction, sewer replacement/rehabilitation, storm water, and nonpoint sources.

The State Revolving Fund was authorized in 1987 to finance a range of environmental projects, and replaced the Construction Grants program. Under the program, EPA provides grants or "seed money" to all 50 states, Puerto Rico, and the District of Columbia to capitalize state loan funds. The states, in turn, make loans to communities and others for high priority water quality activities. As money is paid back into the revolving fund, new loans are made to other recipients. Through June 30, 2000, the program had more than $34 billion in assets and had lent $28.9 billion to communities nationwide. However, only $2.1 billion of that funding had been provided for CSO projects. CSO loans in 2000 were the highest ever, accounting for $411 million, or about 12 percent, of total State Revolving Fund assistance.

Even if a State Revolving Fund loan is obtained, most of the money for water pollution controls must be generated locally. Typically, operational costs are generated from user fees, usually water and sewage treatment charges. There are various options for capital improvements: (1) property taxes; (2) special assessments; (3) tax increment financing; (4) water and sewer hook-up fees; (5) water and sewer use charges; and (6) advanced sale charges for sewer capacity. As noted in Table 3.2, which addresses the four states visited in Region 5, only a small portion (4.2 percent) of CSO needs since 1996 were met by State Revolving Fund loans issued since 1994:

State	Loan Funds Since 1994 (millions)	1996 Needs Amount (millions)	Percentage of 1996 CSO Needs Met
Illinois	$157	$ 9,383	1.7%
Indiana	376	4,463	8.4%
Michigan	300	3,723	8.1%
Ohio	71	4,199	1.7%
Total	$904	$ 21,768	4.2%

Table 3.2: Loan Funding and Needs Met

To maximize the number of projects receiving loans, states have put caps on the amount that can be provided to any one community or project in a given year. However, larger municipalities say this does not allow them to receive enough money for their large projects, while smaller communities expressed concern that they still do not receive enough money. Also, caps varied from state to state. For example, in Michigan, the cap was 30 percent, while in Massachusetts it was 20 percent.

Another aspect of the State Revolving Fund that concerned communities was that many CSO-associated costs are not eligible in some states. For example, the Fund does not pay for telemetry monitoring of the sewer system, project performance certification, lawn restoration, water main replacement, street paving, sewer repair, and studying and planning the project. Port Huron, Michigan officials estimated that costs for studying and planning account for approximately 5 to 10 percent of the total project cost. Springfield, Vermont officials stated that purchase of capital equipment such as vactors (machines that vacuum debris and grit from sewers and catch basins) and sweepers should be eligible items under the

State Revolving Fund program. State Agencies, rather than EPA, determine eligibility of program costs.

Regional and state staff advised us that some communities may not seek State Revolving Fund loans in the hope that a CSO grant program will be established or Congressional earmarks provided. Obviously, most communities would prefer receiving grant funds to having to repay a loan. In particular, economically distressed communities that cannot afford the debt service that would be required to finance a costly CSO project may be especially in need of grant funds.

In Michigan, some economically distressed communities in rural areas have sought funding administered by the U.S. Department of Agriculture for their CSO needs instead of State Revolving Fund loans. These communities found the advantages to be a mix of grant and loan funding and longer repayment periods (40 years for Agriculture as opposed to 20 years for the State Revolving Fund). However, sometimes such funding is not advantageous, since the repayment period can be longer than the useful life of the project.

Finding Suitable Sites Can Also Be an Obstacle

The second major barrier to meeting EPA's CSO remediation goals involves finding acceptable locations for CSO facilities. In many of the communities we visited, such issues as land availability, community opposition, competing land usage (including economic development), and land ownership had complicated matters. Communities' abilities to design or construct CSO projects can be affected by whether there is somewhere to place these projects. CSO projects often involve dedicating large parcels of land for retention basins and other structures. At times, these need to be situated at or close to the waterfront, which is property that is often valuable.

Communities can be stymied in implementing their CSO control projects because of a lack of available land. For example, Garden City, Michigan cannot meet the Michigan Department of Environmental Quality maximum allowable flow of 24.1 cubic feet per second for its system. The city's current projected peak flow is 70 cubic feet per second. To reduce the flow, the city may have to build a large retention basin (for $57 million) or a tunnel (for $47 million). However, the city does not have available land to build either, let alone money to finance the project.

Community opposition is also a barrier to CSO projects. We will discuss some successful approaches to this issue in Chapter 4. Citizens may voice concerns about CSO projects because they have not been educated about the importance and benefit of the project, they are concerned with the loss of park land or other recreational facilities, and they may have a "not-in-my-backyard" opinion. We encountered several of these scenarios during our visits. For example, the Massachusetts Water Resources Authority proposed to construct a pumping facility on vacant land next to an existing power plant and pier. Due to neighborhood opposition, the design work was halted in January 2000. An alternative site suggested by the neighborhood was not available. The status of the project was described in the Authority's annual plan as "design on hold pending project reassessment."

In some cases, communities had to make compromises in their original plans to site their projects. In Detroit there was not enough available land for needed CSO facilities. Occasionally, the city was faced with taking court action to obtain a needed site. In other cases, facilities would have to be put at less advantageous locations and at greater expense because of existing buildings, industries, etc. For example, the Hubbell-Southfield retention facility (see Figure 3.1) was intended to handle a 1-year, 1-hour storm for a duration of 30 minutes. However, because of location constraints and land availability (the site is surrounded by the Tournament of Players Championship Golf Course and the Rouge River), the facility can only handle this type of storm for a duration of 18 minutes. As a result, this biggest of the Rouge River demonstration projects was designed not based on a particular storm event but to fit the largest possible basin on the land available. In another example, New Haven, Connecticut officials said siting could be an issue because they propose to build underground storage tanks on park land, which could disrupt or close the parks for 2 years.

Figure 3.1: Hubbell-Southfield Retention Facility Overflow Gates

Also, since CSO projects may take years to develop, an area initially planned as part of the project may become more desirable later as a result of economic development, and is no longer affordable. Waterfront property in South Boston was identified as an example. Also, in our prior January 2001 report, we noted that the Hudson River waterfront areas in Hoboken and Weehawken, New Jersey had recently undergone explosive growth, and the developers had been reluctant to grant easements to the local authority to access CSO outfalls. There were concerns over siting, CSO control facilities, and the use of end-of-pipe netting in areas where high-priced residences were being constructed.

Conclusion

There are two main barriers that communities face and need to overcome in reducing CSOs and the water pollution they cause. The most significant is financial - there is presently not enough funding to meet the needs of all CSO communities and many communities are being financially strained. A second major barrier involves finding acceptable locations for CSO facilities, due to such complicating factors as land availability, community opposition, competing land usage, and land ownership.

Chapter 4
Many Promising Practices Used by States and Communities Have Improved CSO Program

States and communities have demonstrated a wide variety of cost effective and promising practices that could be used by others with CSO programs to address funding and siting barriers. In Chapter 3, we noted that raising and obtaining sufficient funding for expensive capital projects was the largest barrier to the success of the national CSO program. We found that some states have or are considering assisting their communities with direct financial aid through grant programs. Local governments are educating their citizens on the benefits of CSO programs and the need to raise sewer rates to fund these projects. Locally, it was also found that improving community facilities and working cooperatively with other agencies to minimize disruptions can be beneficial. Additionally, communities brought to our attention various technical practices that can improve system efficiency and aid in making CSO projects more affordable.

Table 4.1 describes the relationship between the types of promising practices and the barriers CSO communities face.

Barriers	Practices
Funding	State Grants Coordination/Cooperation Technical
Funding, Siting	Education Dissemination
Siting	Improved Facility

Table 4.1: Barriers Addressed by Promising Practices

State Grant Programs Aid Affordability

Two of the eight states we visited have established CSO grant programs to help communities pay for the construction of CSO projects in a more timely manner. A third state was considering implementing a grant program.

Connecticut established its CSO grant program in 1986. The program provided grants for 50 percent of the Federal eligible project costs along with a State Revolving Fund loan at 2 percent interest for the remainder of the costs. Since 1988 Connecticut awarded $173 million to eight municipalities.

The Director of Engineering and Planning at the Hartford Metropolitan District Commission stated the program had a positive impact on debt service and made CSO abatement a viable program, since independently Hartford could not issue $80 million in debt. The Assistant General Manager of the New Haven Water Pollution Control Authority also said that the grant/loan program made the CSO projects more affordable and had a positive impact on user rates. Without the funds, New Haven's water rates would go beyond EPA's affordability cap. The Assistant General Manager further said that the Authority was able to do more projects more quickly and, without the funding, would not be able to meet the 12-15 year time frame provided in its long-term control plan.

Vermont awarded 25-percent grants for construction costs and loans of 50 percent of eligible project costs from the State Revolving Fund. The remaining 25 percent was expected to be locally raised. Grants through fiscal 2000 totaled $6.6 million. The Springfield Town Manager stated that without the grant funds it would be hard to sell a CSO project to the voters for approval. The town had recently finished a $4 million project for which it received $1 million in state grant funds and a 50-percent loan at close to zero-percent interest. The Rutland Commissioner of Public Works also stated that grant funds were beneficial and helped keep user rates down.

Pennsylvania was also considering a CSO grant program. Pennsylvania's General Assembly introduced Senate Bill 150 on January 29, 2001, to establish a grant program to assist municipalities in addressing CSO impacts. The bill proposes approving $1 billion for the program.

Educating the Public Reaps Benefits

The public does not always understand the benefits to be derived from CSO projects that may significantly raise their user rates and require temporary or permanent disruption of land use. Public officials in turn may not be willing to counter public sentiment. Therefore, communities found that it was important to engage and inform their stakeholders early and maintain communication throughout the CSO project process. Education is a vital tool that can eliminate potential barriers or opposition related to funding and siting, provide support for the project, and reduce overall costs and disruptions. Many state and local officials stated that public education is important because the public is usually more willing to pay for improvements it can see and understand. For example:

A Rouge River Public Involvement Action Plan was devised in the fall of 1994. The goal was to engage numerous stakeholders, inform them, gain their support, and encourage them to change their behavior to help achieve and maintain a healthy watershed. A series of fact sheets and brochures were prepared for the general public as well as for a more technical audience regarding different elements of the Project. Printed materials were distributed with a portable display; provided to local governments to distribute; and incorporated into public information packets for local officials, the general public, libraries, and schools. A June 1998 Project report on lessons learned noted that broad-based public education and involvement programs were critical for overall success. Some of the programs that they found had worked were: getting education programs going in area schools; getting people out to the stream to look at and experience it; and showing people some obvious things that have been done to get successes in improved water quality and then widely publicizing the results.

Hartford, Connecticut developed a public education campaign that helped the successful passage of a referendum for funding part of its CSO project.

New Haven, Connecticut issued a series of newsletters explaining CSO plans, costs, and benefits to city aldermen and local environmental groups. The city found that educating local public officials about CSO needs eased local constituency concerns.

Springfield, Vermont officials visited schools and local groups, such as garden/sewing clubs, to explain why CSO abatement was important and deserving of town funding. Town officials worked with local media to take pictures and report on the issue.

Ohio roundtable participants stated that by focusing on basement flooding issues that directly affected residences and businesses, they were able to sell CSO projects to the public. Citizens could better understand and appreciate how the projects could immediately benefit them.

Toledo, Ohio worked with the children living in the Maumee River basin by having school children take water samples and do stream cleanups, thus learning the importance of protecting their receiving stream.

Improved Community Facilities Can Result

The final constructed project can be aesthetically pleasing and bring improved facilities to the local community in which it's built. Neighborhood opposition to the siting of a CSO project can be overcome when citizens are convinced there can be benefits to the community in addition to the obvious environmental ones. We visited a number of facilities in the Rouge River Project that demonstrated this fact.

Wayne County had three retention facilities constructed as part of the Rouge River National Demonstration Project. The Redford Township CSO Retention Basin was constructed under the seventh hole of the Glenhurst Golf Course. The Dearborn Heights CSO Retention Basin was constructed on a landfill that was subsequently landscaped with a soccer field, gazebo, bicycle rack, and parking. The Inkster CSO Retention Basin added multiple-use recreational facilities (basketball court and playground equipment) on top of the storage tank (see Figure 4.1). All three constructed attractive buildings to house any above ground machinery.

Figure 4.1: Recreational Facility Sitting on Top of the Inkster CSO Retention Basin

Figure 4.2: Control Building (Birmingham Hills) Retention Basin

Oakland County also blended its three Rouge River retention basins into the local environs. One was built under a golf course, another was built in a nature preserve, and the third was built in a park. The latter one (Birmingham Hills) had a control building that was designed to resemble a gristmill (see Figure 4.2). Also, extensive woodlands landscaping was completed to blend with the aesthetics of the site. County officials even described how a real estate agent had stopped by and wanted to list the house.

Government Agency Cooperation Achieves Better Results

To address the funding barrier, communities found that working cooperatively with state offices or coordinating between appropriate municipal departments can improve the planning process, reduce costs, lessen disruptions, and increase timeliness of project completion.

In Michigan, officials for Michigan Department of Environmental Quality noted the value of involving everyone who might have an interest or stake in the project. They found that integrating state offices (i.e., Michigan Department of Transportation) and city offices (i.e., a local Office of Development) at the beginning of a CSO project significantly reduced costs and disruptions. Port Huron officials reported saving money by coordinating their work with road repairs conducted by the state Department of Transportation. Lansing officials reported that constant and frequent communication with the regulatory community, homeowners, businesses, and other city and state departments resulted in less confusion, better planning, and better project understanding.

Ohio roundtable participants stated that the coordination of CSO projects with other major construction projects, as well as with state or Federal agencies, had minimized disruptions.

Better Technical Practices

The municipalities visited implemented some technical practices and approaches that can be beneficial to other CSO communities. They ranged from broad-based initiatives to more specific operational actions. While these practices cannot necessarily be universally used, they offer opportunities to lessen financial needs or improve Combined Sewer System efficiency and effectiveness, and can assist communities in addressing affordability issues. Following are some success stories:

- The Rouge River Project, which involved 48 communities in the Detroit, Michigan metropolitan area, provided several examples of better practices of a technical nature. Under Phase I, 8 communities constructed 10 retention treatment basins. Each basin was sized for different storm events, and several used innovative technology. The facilities also incorporated a variety of additional features or variations in compartment sizing and sequencing (such as a first-flush chamber) to improve effectiveness. From this approach, the Rouge River Project team determined that desired water quality results could be achieved without constructing massive facilities. In addition, the lessons learned by comparing the various methodologies will assist Rouge River Project communities in the design of future CSO facilities and reduce project costs.

  Another lesson learned from the Rouge River Project was that it was beneficial for plant operators to be involved in the entire facility design process. By obtaining their input, they were able to point out a variety of issues to the design engineers that avoided the need for future modifications. Additionally, operators seemed to perform better and with higher morale because they were members of the design team and their ideas were valued and implemented by the designers.

- Hartford, Connecticut applied the concept of flow slipping in the Wethersfield Cove drainage basin area. The concept involves reducing street ponding during wet weather events. Flow slipping allows storm water runoff to bypass the CSO catch basins and flow directly to newly constructed storm water catch basins (separated storm drains). Hartford saved money by not having to: (1) construct catch basins on every street and (2) treat all the storm water collected. It should be noted that flow slipping is topographically limited and cannot be used everywhere.

- The Massachusetts Water Resources Authority (the water and sewer agency for greater Boston) used underflow baffles for floatable control. These baffles (barriers) are used to prevent floatable material (such as plastic bags, straws, bottles, bottle caps, and cigarette butts) from entering the system and ending up in the receiving water body.

- Springfield, Vermont addressed affordability when it reduced the amount of salt/sand it uses in winter. The town used a spreader that reduced the amount of salt/sand by 30 to 40 percent without reducing road clearing effectiveness. This approach reduces the material that can build up in the sewer system and reduce flow capacity.

- Rutland, Vermont and New Bedford, Massachusetts both described aggressive preventive maintenance programs, including such techniques as TV inspections of sewer lines, cleaning of sewer lines and catch basins, and street cleaning. Such actions improved system effectiveness and reduced overall operating costs.

- Paulding, Ohio cleaned its existing wastewater treatment lagoons to increase their capacity to handle CSOs. City officials said that, as a result, the city avoided having to construct costly CSO retention basins to contain the storm water.

- Crafton, Pennsylvania bought and maintained undeveloped land to act as a buffer to receiving waters by absorbing runoff. In addition, Crafton maintained about 25 percent of its streets as brick, which has water absorption qualities as well as historical and aesthetic value. Further, Crafton bought additional trash barrels, which helped reduce street trash and subsequent floatables.

Dissemination of Better Practices Needed

There currently is no central mechanism for EPA or the states to disseminate information to CSO permittees about the various better practices that are being used. EPA's CSO Coordinator stated that there is a need to develop a plan to establish a technology clearinghouse.

During our evaluation, we found many instances where communities were unaware of established practices that could be of benefit to them. We provided them with examples from other municipalities we had visited and contacts to seek further information. For example, we provided the Defiance, Ohio Water

Pollution Control Superintendent with contacts in Port Huron, Lansing, and New Bedford to discuss their CSO control activities.

Individual websites do exist where some information can be obtained. Several examples are noted in Table 4.2:

Source	Website
Massachusetts Water Resources Authority	www.mwra.com
3 Rivers Project	www.3riverswetweather.org
Rouge River Project	www.wcdoe.org/rougeriver

Table 4.2: Websites with Best Practices Information

Rouge River Project officials also met with officials from many CSO communities to discuss the project and the actions taken. Information is also exchanged at seminars and meetings that professional organizations hold throughout the year. However, there is no one place where interested parties can find all the available information.

Conclusion

States and communities have demonstrated a number of promising practices to address the funding and siting barriers that are faced in implementing the CSO Policy. Two New England states have aggressively addressed the affordability issue by providing grants and low interest loans. There is also widespread agreement that public education is a vital tool in engaging all stakeholders. Additionallly, communities have shown that the cooperative effort of all levels of government can be beneficial. Further, communities have used innovative approaches to improve CSO controls and make them more efficient and/or cost effective. However, with all these positive actions, there needs to be a central mechanism so that other CSO communities take advantage of this wisdom.

Recommendation

We recommend that the Assistant Administrator for Water ensure that:

4.1 EPA develop a system to catalog and disseminate lessons learned and better practices about CSOs. EPA should establish a website where such information can be posted and information easily accessed for use.

Chapter 5
Limited Data Available on Improvements to Water Quality

The CSO communities visited had varying amounts and types of data available to determine the success of their CSO projects. Most communities were only monitoring the number, volume, and duration of CSO discharges. Few of the communities visited had formally collected data on the effect CSO controls were having on the quality of receiving waters. Without such data, it could not be determined whether each project was a wise investment of taxpayers' dollars. Water quality generally was not monitored because EPA policy does not require monitoring until completion of the CSO project, even though these projects have multiple steps and can take years to complete.

CSO Policy Requires Monitoring Program

During long-term control plan development, the CSO Policy expects CSO communities to collect data to assess baseline conditions in the receiving water and evaluate the potential effectiveness of any proposed controls in improving water quality and supporting uses of the water body. Permittees are expected to develop a comprehensive, representative monitoring program that measures the frequency, duration, flow rate, volume, and pollutant concentration of CSO discharges and assesses CSO impact on receiving waters. The Policy also calls for a post-construction compliance monitoring program that verifies compliance with water quality standards and protection of designated uses and ascertains the effectiveness of CSO controls.

Many Communities Did Not Have Monitoring Data

We found that most communities had limited monitoring data on the effect of CSO controls they instituted on water quality. These communities generally only measured the changes in the number, volume, and duration of effluent being discharged by CSOs. This was because they had not completed their CSO projects. As noted in Chapter 2, EPA recently reported that only 34 percent of CSO communities in its review had even submitted draft long-term control plans to states for approval. Once approvals are issued, complete implementation of these plans can take 10 to 15 years. Since many communities do not plan to perform monitoring until the post-construction phase, there is limited knowledge of the effects of CSO controls on water quality.

For example, Connecticut Department of Environmental Protection officials stated that they were not aware of any studies to indicate whether CSO abatement efforts had improved water quality in CSO receiving waters. Officials from the three Connecticut cities we visited confirmed that they had not conducted any CSO water quality monitoring. Connecticut's State Revolving Fund had loaned out about $75 million for CSO projects since 1987.

Vermont was another New England state where CSO communities indicated they had not conducted any CSO water quality monitoring. Officials in both Rutland and Springfield stated that they had not done any measurements of water quality related to CSOs. Vermont Department of Environmental Conservation officials stated that communities were required to submit an assessment of the success of long-term control plan implementation. Vermont's State Revolving Fund had loaned out about $37 million for CSO projects since 1987.

In Pennsylvania, the Executive Director of the 3 Rivers Demonstration Project stated that there were not enough controls in place yet to measure water quality because their work was not far enough along. Allegheny County Sanitary Authority officials also stated that water monitoring will not take place until the long-term control plan is implemented.

Some Communities Do Monitor Water Quality

Several of the CSO communities we visited had performed extensive monitoring and had data to show that water quality had improved since the implementation of CSO controls.

The Rouge River Project had an extensive monitoring program. It was performed in conjunction with the Michigan Department of Environmental Quality's August 1998 *Final Criteria for Success in CSO Treatment.* The criteria noted, "We expect to develop criteria for success in treating CSO discharges statewide, based on experience gained from the Rouge River demonstration project." The criteria set three goals and a detailed listing of procedures to evaluate the goals and information that was to be reported. For example, the final goal was to achieve state water quality standards in the receiving stream at times of discharge.

An extensive database on water quality was also compiled by Toledo, Ohio since 1968 as part of the city's Water Quality Monitoring program. This program produced a detailed study of CSO impacts. The information was used to plan major upgrades of the city's treatment and interceptor system. In addition, the program developed abatement criteria and documented the benefits of Toledo's abatement program. Recent results highlighted improved water quality when the post-abatement period was compared to the pre-abatement period.

Since 1989, the Massachusetts Water Resources Authority has been implementing a water quality sampling plan required as part of a Federal court order for the Boston Harbor cleanup. Data were collected and analyzed for bacteria.

CSO Projects Did Improve Water Quality

While elimination of CSOs may not necessarily assure water quality standards are attained, there still is evidence investments in CSO remediation has resulted in declines in discharges and, at least in some cases, water quality has improved.

Declines in Discharges

Communities we visited generally measured changes in the number, volume, and duration of effluent being discharged by CSOs:

- **Number:** The number of discharge events for the Rouge River in Michigan was reduced by 80 percent.

- **Volume:** Port Huron, Michigan, at the completion of construction in 2002, will have reduced CSO volume from 226 to 114 million gallons per year (52 percent).

- **Duration:** A West Lafayette, Indiana sewer project eliminated one CSO point that resulted in 484 yearly hours of CSOs being reduced to 20 hours (96-percent reduction).

Water Quality Improvements

When data existed, improvements to water quality were noted after the implementation of CSO abatement programs. The following are several examples of the successes that have resulted in measurable water quality improvements.

- Michigan Department of Environmental Quality data demonstrated that three Oakland County and three Wayne County CSO retention basins eliminate raw sewage and protect public health. Also, the three Oakland County basins met the dissolved oxygen and physical characteristics water quality standards.

- In areas with remaining uncontrolled CSOs upstream on the Rouge River, data showed dramatic improvements in the river's dissolved oxygen levels because of upstream CSO control projects and other watershed management changes. For example, on the Main Rouge River, the dissolved oxygen data for the water quality standards show that the dissolved oxygen levels improved from 40 percent below water quality standards in 1998 to 5 percent in 2000. Also, on the Lower Rouge River, the dissolved oxygen levels dropped from 70 percent below standards in 1994 to 4 percent in 2000.
- Water quality in the Swan Creek and Maumee River in Toledo, Ohio, had been upgraded. Minimum dissolved oxygen levels, maximum fecal coliform levels, and aesthetics had improved. Also, Toledo reported an increase of game fish in Swan Creek, and a 75-percent capture rate of CSOs in the city's central business district.

- The Massachusetts Water Resources Authority, in its October 6, 2000 report, *Statistical Analysis of Combined Sewer Overflow Receiving Water Data, 1989-1999*, concluded that a significant and detectable decline in bacterial concentrations in Boston area receiving waters since 1991 had occurred. Specifically, all of the regions with data for the before and after improvement periods – including Dorchester Bay, the Neponset River, the Inner Harbor, the Mystic River, and the Charles River – showed significant reduction in the number of indicator organisms since 1991. The Inner Harbor, Mystic River, and Charles River showed a steady and significant decline in both fecal coliform and enteroccocci concentrations on a year-to-year basis. The report also noted that there tended to be a correlation between rainfall events and bacterial concentrations in the Boston Harbor area CSO receiving waters over the years of sampling.

- New Bedford, Massachusetts opened 5,000 acres of shellfish beds that had been closed for 30 to 40 years.

Conclusion

We found that few CSO communities were collecting data on the effect that CSO controls were having on the water quality of their receiving waters. Most communities were monitoring the loadings as opposed to the water quality itself. Therefore, they generally used information on the number, volume, and duration of CSO events to determine the effectiveness of their actions. Data was not expected to be collected, in these cases, until the post-construction phase, which could be 10 to 15 years in the future. We believe it is important to do interim monitoring throughout the process to ensure CSO efforts were being effective and improving water quality.

Recommendation

We recommend that the Assistant Administrator for Water:

5.1 Work with CSO permitting authorities and communities to assure they negotiate and establish the proper level of interim monitoring of CSO efforts to determine the impact of the project on water quality.

Chapter 6
CSO Efforts Need to Focus More on Entire Watershed

While CSO discharges are a significant pollution source for many water bodies, eliminating them will not always ensure that water quality standards will be met. Other major sources contributing to water body degradation can include sanitary sewer overflows, storm water, pollution from upstream sources (including nonpoint), and concentrated animal feeding operations. Therefore, while many communities spend large sums to alleviate their CSO problems, communities should focus on all problems for a watershed – not just CSOs – in order to effectively improve water quality. In most watersheds, the sources of water quality problems are too varied to be amenable to a single solution. Further, communities should also ensure that water quality standards in place are appropriate and attainable.

Many Factors Impact Water Quality

For many communities, upstream or downstream pollution may overwhelm any pollution reductions they can achieve through CSO elimination efforts. Eliminating CSOs may achieve only a marginal improvement in water quality. While some communities may be able to eliminate all of their water quality problems by eliminating their CSOs, that is generally the exception rather than the rule. For most water bodies that currently fail to meet water quality standards, there are multiple causes.

The Association of Metropolitan Sewerage Agencies, in its February 2002 report, supported this viewpoint. In a survey of its members, 78 percent of respondents indicated that water quality standards would not always be met during wet weather conditions after full implementation of the CSO long-term control plan. The report also suggested that, "parallel efforts to address other controlled and uncontrolled upstream sources must be greatly expanded."

The difficulty in achieving water quality standards by eliminating CSOs was also voiced by many of the communities we visited. Examples follow:

- A Massachusetts Water Resources Authority report, *Beyond the Boston Harbor Project 1997-1998, The State of Boston Harbor*, noted the results of computer modeling of fecal coliform bacteria levels in Boston Harbor and its tributary rivers after rainstorms. It stated: "Despite the highly controlled CSO discharges called for in MWRA's (Massachusetts Water Resources Authority's) CSO Plan, river water quality is still predicted to be poor after rainstorms because of storm water input."

- West Lafayette, Indiana officials indicated that they could do nothing to change the brownish color of their receiving waters, which is caused by pollution from nonpoint sources and concentrated animal feeding operations located upstream.

- Perrysburg, Ohio officials had not seen any visible change in the Maumee River since they implemented CSO controls. They said that the river was significantly impacted by agricultural runoff, and water quality objectives might be better achieved by regulating the agricultural industry. The EPA 1998 Water Quality Inventory report listed agriculture as one of several leading sources of pollutants in four of our visited states (Ohio, Illinois, Indiana, and Michigan).

- Officials in Hartford and New Haven, Connecticut, as well as Haverhill, Massachusetts, pointed to pollution from communities upstream of their cities as hindering their ability to meet water quality standards.

This interrelationship of pollution sources was not always something that community leaders were aware of. It was at times assumed that the expensive CSO control projects would alleviate water quality issues.

Watershed Approach Should Be Considered

Because of the wide variety of pollution sources affecting urban waters and their impact on communities, we believe CSO control should be viewed in the context of watershed management. In particular, many of the receiving water measures and ecological, human health, and resource use measures quantify impacts or effects that are often governed by sources beyond CSOs. We believe, as do many in the CSO community, that attaining water quality standards and meeting designated uses can only be accomplished through a concerted effort to limit all sources of pollutants. However, this approach should not delay necessary CSO initiatives within the watershed context.

The watershed approach is built on three main principles. First, the target watersheds should be those where pollution poses the greatest risk to human health, ecological resources, desirable use of the water, or a combination of these. Second, all parties with a stake in the watershed should participate in the analysis of problems and the creation of solutions. Third, the actions undertaken should draw upon the full range of methods and tools available, integrating them into a coordinated, multi-organization attack on the problems.

Rouge River Project a Blueprint for Success

The Rouge River National Wet Weather Demonstration in Michigan is an excellent example of how utilizing a watershed approach can help to achieve water quality goals more efficiently. We have previously described in this report some of the successful results that have been achieved by this project.

Recognizing the major costs involved in controlling CSOs and that other sources of pollution impacted water quality, Congress appropriated money in 1992 to establish the Rouge River Project. The total funds earmarked by Congress for the Project has reached $346.8 million. The Rouge River watershed is largely urbanized, spans approximately 438 square miles, and is home to over 1.5 million people in 48 communities and three counties, including Detroit.

Rouge River Project officials stated that water quality has to be dealt with on a macro level. Solutions can be better derived from a holistic watershed perspective. Communities should not work separately, and are more productive if they work together. In this way, consideration is given to the inter-relationship between the impacts from all sources of pollution and use impairments in a receiving water. Project officials also stated that the watershed approach was cost beneficial for participating communities and ultimately resulted in greater and faster achievement of designated uses in a water body. Further, Project officials stated that progress on the project had shown that use of a watershed approach did not mean delay, and action could be taken on CSO controls and other abatement initiatives within the context of a watershed approach.

While we applaud the many successes that have been achieved through the Rouge River Project, we recognize that there were some advantageous factors that increased the possibility of success. First, Congress provided massive direct funding to assist communities in the construction of the expensive CSO projects. Second, the entire project was located within one state's jurisdiction. Many other watershed opportunities may involve multi-state issues, which can make coordination and management more difficult.

Others Recognize Need for Watershed Approach

Other CSO communities and interested parties have recognized the need for a watershed approach to address water quality issues. For example, communities in the three EPA Regions we reviewed (Regions 1, 3, and 5) have begun to work collectively to address common problems.

- Massachusetts and New Hampshire communities along the Merrimack River have joined together to form the Merrimack CSO Coalition. The participating communities believed it was in their best interest to form a coalition to address the impact of CSOs and other pollutants on the river. They further believed that a coalition would strengthen their collective ability to influence regulatory agencies toward a more creative, comprehensive and effective approach to improving the affected waters.

- In Pennsylvania, the 3 Rivers Wet Weather Demonstration Program divided the Allegheny County Sanitary Authority's 83 communities into 8 planning basins that share sewersheds. In early 2001, three basin groups had been formed. The basin groups consisted of elected and appointed officials from each community in the basin. Each group's purpose was to plan and implement collaborative projects that will benefit municipalities by combining financial and technical resources while proactively working to comply with the Clean Water Act. The Chartiers Basin Group Chair, who was from a town of about 7,000 people, stated that this combined approach was important because a community of his size could not address these issues alone.

- Several municipalities on the Maumee River in Indiana and Ohio recently formed the Maumee River Basin Partnership of Local Governments to address watershed issues (see map). The Partnership, announced in March 2001, has begun to provide a collective resource and forum where city, town, and county officials can share vital water quality information and enhance their regional communication efforts. For example, in June 2001, the Partnership formed a Regulatory Issues Working Group whose focus includes Federal CSO funding issues, total maximum daily loads, NPDES permitting, and concentrated animal feeding operations.

The Association of Metropolitan Sewerage Agencies, in a February 2002 report,

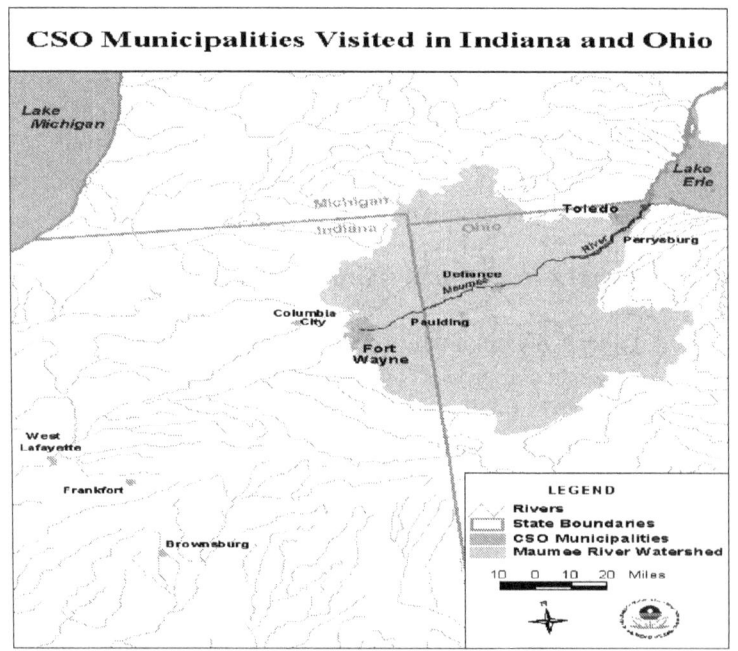

The National Response to Combined Sewer Overflows, stated that it had long sought the ability to address wet weather pollution problems in accordance with watershed management principles. The organization believed that a comprehensive approach would result in a systematic, incremental, and more cost-effective achievement of water quality objectives.

EPA Favors Watershed Approach

All of this supports EPA's long-held position on the subject. EPA has been in favor of watershed approaches for over a decade. In 1991, the Office of Water issued the *Watershed Protection Approach Framework*. In June 1996, EPA explained its vision of watershed approaches and built on the 1991 document with the *Watershed Approach Framework*. In the cover letter to that document, the EPA Administrator stated, "We believe the watershed approach can significantly improve water resource restoration, protection and maintenance and achieve lasting environmental results."

Further, in its December 2001 report to Congress, EPA indicated that the attainment of water quality standards could not often be achieved solely through CSO controls because of other point and nonpoint sources. The report stated that the integration of long-term control plan development in a watershed context would alleviate some concerns about meeting water quality standards and equity.

Even though EPA advocates a watershed approach, it still administers its water programs categorically. A recent draft EPA review of state programs pointed out that, "States identified a number of barriers posed by EPA and federal authorities to implementing... watershed management" including "fragmented and output-oriented" oversight of state programs.

Recently, EPA began focusing on the goal of integrating the NPDES program further into the concept of watershed planning. EPA is exploring models for a watershed permitting program that would allow for local leadership in conducting watershed planning and selecting appropriate management options to meet watershed goals and Clean Water Act requirements.

Appropriate and Attainable Water Quality Standards Needed

According to EPA staff, one of the "major" issues causing CSO implementation to lag was the lack of water quality standards reviews during the CSO planning process. One key principle, which ensures that CSO controls are cost-effective and meet the objective of the Clean Water Act, is the "review and revision as appropriate, of water quality standards and their implementation procedures when developing CSO control plans to reflect the site-specific wet weather impacts of CSOs." On July 31, 2001, EPA issued *Guidance: Coordinating CSO Long-Term Planning with Water Quality Standards Reviews*, because "in the 7 years since EPA issued the CSO Control Policy, implementation of this principle has not progressed as quickly as expected." This lack of progress was due in part to a reluctance by regulatory agencies, environmental groups, public officials, and the public to accept what is perceived as the downgrading of water quality standards. The review process can be so intensive as to become burdensome.

Nationwide, only the Massachusetts Water Resources Authority obtained a variance from water quality standards for CSOs. A variance is a discharge-specific, short-term modification to the applicable water quality standard, typically of 3- to 5-year duration. When a state adopts the variance, it must have sufficient data to determine that the designated use is not attainable within the duration of the variance.

It is up to the states to propose a revision to water quality standards. They make this proposal by submitting a use attainability analysis to the public and EPA. A use attainability analysis is a structured scientific assessment of the physical, chemical, biological, and economic factors affecting the attainment of the use for a water body. The detailed water quality, financial, and technical information needed for the use attainability analysis can be required as part of the scope of a community's long-term control plan. The study costs are part of the CSO planning process, which can range from a few hundred thousand dollars to millions. Public participation should be a part of the process. If appropriate, the state submits to EPA a proposal to change water quality standards.

While the use attainability analysis process is the means for revising a water body's designated use, it is usually a contentious process. For example, the Massachusetts Department of Environmental Protection's CSO Coordinator described the use attainability analysis process as "onerous," noting, "lowering a water quality standard is rarely warmly received either by the regulatory agencies or with watershed advocacy groups or politicians. The process can be contentious at times, with lengthy debate over costs, CSO controls, receiving water goals and conditions."

Generally, the CSO Partnership officials stated that more realistic water quality standards need to be developed. The CSO Partnership believed that some states' definition of fishable and swimmable waters was a barrier because not all streams are fishable or swimmable 365 days a year due to wet weather conditions (people should not expect to swim in waters after a rain storm). EPA's December 2001 report to Congress also noted this concern that most states use fishable/swimmable as their default-designated use.

In commenting on EPA's draft guidance on reviewing water quality standards with long-term control plan development, the CSO Partnership wrote, "The States need a strong and clear commitment from EPA that EPA will support their efforts and will provide the political support (based upon scientific realities) necessary to allow refinements in designated uses and water quality standards for urban CSO receiving waters." In the opinion of the CSO Partnership's counsel, EPA's final guidance was too intimidating for many communities and EPA needed to show, through demonstration projects, how to implement the guidance.

EPA's Office of Science and Technology held a national symposium in June 2002 to hear stakeholder views on designated use. At its conclusion, EPA decided it will develop guidance for recreational use, with subsequent guides on other uses.

Conclusion

It needs to be recognized that eliminating CSOs by themselves may not necessarily assure the attainment of water quality standards. Receiving waters can still be degraded by other sources, including pollution from various point and nonpoint sources such as sanitary sewer overflows, storm water, and concentrated animal feeding operations. To address the broad variety of pollution sources that affect water bodies, EPA has been encouraging a watershed approach. We found examples where the watershed approach has been successful when dealing with CSO issues, and believe its use should be expanded.

Also, CSO communities were not taking advantage of the flexibility that the CSO Policy afforded them in undertaking water quality standards reviews during the CSO planning process. This lack of progress was due in part to a reluctance by regulatory agencies, environmental groups, public officials, and the public to accept what is perceived as the downgrading of water quality standards. In addition, the review process can be so intensive as to become burdensome.

Recommendations

We recommend that the Assistant Administrator for Water:

6.1 Provide a leadership role by working with states and communities to develop watershed approaches that will target priority activities and will ensure that water quality standards are met.

6.2 Provide a leadership role by encouraging states and communities to work with other stakeholders to develop appropriate water quality standards and, when appropriate, revise those standards.

6.3 Encourage states to adopt water quality standards recognizing seasonal recreational uses.

Exhibit 1
Nine Minimum Controls and Long-Term Control Plans

Nine Minimum Controls

As noted in the EPA's May 31, 1995, "Guidance For Nine Minimum Controls," there are controls that can reduce CSOs and their effects on water quality. They do not require major engineering studies and usually can be implemented in less than 2 years. The nine minimum controls are as follows:

- Proper operations and regular maintenance programs for the sewer system and CSO outfalls.

- Maximum use of the collection system for storage.

- Review and modification of pretreatment requirements to ensure that CSO impact are minimized.

- Maximization of flow to the publically-owned treatment works for treatment.

- Elimination of CSOs during dry weather.

- Control of solid and floatable materials in CSOs.

- Pollution prevention programs to reduce contaminants in CSOs.

- Public notification to ensure that the public receives adequate notification of CSO occurrences and CSO impacts.

- Monitoring to effectively characterize CSO impacts and the efficacy of CSO controls.

These controls are not temporary measures: they should be a part of the CSO's long-term controls. Selection and implementation of actual control measures should be based on site-specific considerations, including the specific characteristics identified in the characterization and monitoring of the combined sewer system.

Long-Term Control Plans

According to the CSO Policy, CSO permittees are responsible for developing and implementing long-term control plans that will ulitimately result in compliance with Clean Water Act requirements. The plans should consider the site-specific nature of CSOs and evaluate the cost effectiveness of a range of control options. The selected controls should be designed to allow for retrofitting or expansion if additional controls become necessary to meet water quality standards, including existing and designated uses. A permittee can use one of two approaches to demonstrate that its selected CSO controls will achieve water quality standards. These are the "presumption" and "demonstration" approaches.

Using the "**presumption**" approach, the permittee provides a specific level of control that is presumed to meet water quality standards. The selection of this approach does not release a permittee from the overall requirement of meeting water quality standards. If the permitting authority determined that the plan will not result in meeting Clean Water Act requirements, then the presumption will not apply. Under the "presumption" approach, controls adopted in the plan should be required to meet one of the following criteria:

- No more than an average of four overflow events per year, provided that the permitting authority may allow up to two additional overflow events per year;

- The elimination or the capture for treatment of no less than 85 percent by volume of the combined sewerage collected in the combined sewer system during precipitation events on a system-wide annual average basis; or

- The elimination of the pollutants or removal of no less that the mass of the pollutants identified as causing water quality impairment through the sewer system characterization, monitoring, and modeling effort for the volumes that would be captured for treatment above.

In the "**demonstration**" approach, the permittee provides information and data that show the selected controls meet the water quality standards and designated uses. In selecting the "demonstration" approach, a community would have several options for developing a long-term control plan. The CSO Policy identifies four criteria for successful use of the "demonstration" approach:

- The CSO control program will protect water quality standards unless the standard cannot be met as a result of natural conditions or other pollution sources;

- The overflows remaining after implementation of the control program will not prevent attainment of water quality standards;

- The planned control program will achieve the maximum pollution reduction benefits reasonably attainable; and

- The planned control program designed to allow cost effective expansion or cost effective retrofitting if additional controls are subsequently determined to be necessary to meet water quality standards, including protection of designated uses.

Exhibit 2
Review Participants

EPA

Office of Wastewater Management (Office of Water)
Great Lakes National Program Office
Region 1
Region 3
Region 5

By State

Connecticut

Connecticut Department of Environmental Protection
City of Bridgeport
City of Hartford
City of New Haven

Illinois

Illinois Environmental Protection Agency
Metropolitan Water Reclamation District of Greater Chicago

Indiana

Indiana Department of Environmental Management
Town of Brownsburg
Columbia City
City of Fort Wayne
City of Frankfort
City of West Lafayette

Massachusetts

Massachusetts Department of Environmental Protection
Massachusetts Water Resources Authority
City of Haverhill
City of New Bedford

Michigan

Michigan Department of Environmental Quality
City of Dearborn
City of Dearborn Heights

City of Detroit
Garden City
City of Lansing
City of Livonia
Oakland County
City of Port Huron
Wayne County
United States District Court Monitor

Ohio

Ohio Environmental Protection Agency
City of Akron
Metropolitan Sewer District of Cincinnati
City of Columbus
City of Defiance
City of Lancaster
City of Lima
City of Newark
Northeast Ohio Regional Sewer District
Village of Paulding
City of Perrysburg
City of Port Clinton
City of Toledo

Pennsylvania

Pennsylvania Department of Environmental Protection
Allegheny County Sanitary Authority
Town of Crafton
City of Pittsburgh
Ross Township
3 Rivers Demonstration Program

Vermont

Vermont Department of Environmental Conservation
City of Rutland
City of Springfield

Organizations

Association of Metropolitan Sewage Agencies
CSO Partnership

Appendix 1
Agency Response

UNITED STATES ENVIRONMENTAL PROTECTION AGENCY
WASHINGTON, D.C. 20460

JUL 1 5 2002

OFFICE OF
WATER

MEMORANDUM

SUBJECT: Draft Report *Wastewater Management: Controlling and Abating Combined Sewer Overflows*

FROM: G. Tracy Mehan, III
Assistant Administrator

TO: Dan Engelberg, Ph.D.
Director for Program Evaluation, Water
Office of Program Evaluation
Office of Inspector General

Thank you for the opportunity to review and comment on your draft report *Wastewater Management: Controlling and Abating Combined Sewer Overflows*.

In general, we agree with many of the findings and recommendations in your draft report. The findings in your draft report, to a large degree, support what we identified in EPA's 2001 *Report to Congress – Implementation and Enforcement of the Combined Sewer Overflow Control Policy*: funding of CSO control programs, promoting and facilitating the review and revision, as appropriate, of water quality standards, and developing a national data system for comprehensively evaluating the implementation and the effectiveness of the CSO control program. You also have identified a number of actions we should take to address the barriers that hinder the control of CSOs. These actions are discussed in the attachment.

Staff in the Office of Wastewater Management (OWM) coordinated the review of the draft report with appropriate staff in Regions 1, 3, and 5. The Regions provided specific comments on the draft report. OWM staff are providing, under separate cover, these comments to Ira Brass of your office. Mr. Brass was the lead investigator in preparing the report. OWM will discuss and address these comments with him. Regional Office staff will participate in these discussions as necessary.

Recycled/Recyclable • Printed with Vegetable Oil Based Inks on 100% Recycled Paper (20% Postconsumer)

If you have any questions about the attached response to the conclusions and recommendations contained in the draft report, please contact me at 202-564-5700 or Linda Boornazian, Director, Water Permits Division, Office of Wastewater Management, at 202-564-9545.

cc: Judy Hecht

Attachment

ATTACHMENT

EPA Responses to Specific Conclusions

Chapter 2 Conclusion: *States and communities have been working for decades addressing CSOs. States in all three regions we visited made efforts to abate CSOs, but not all States set CSO abatement as a high priority, which ultimately delayed progress towards eliminating CSO outfalls. While all States adopted CSO strategies and guidelines, long-term control plan implementations were at different stages.*

EPA Response: The Office of Water generally agrees with this conclusion. When EPA issued the CSO Control Policy in April, 1994, many States had CSO permitting strategies established in response to EPA's 1989 CSO Control Strategy. With the issuance of the Policy, the states adapted their on-going strategies, in varying degrees, to meet the principles of the Policy. A number of States continued to implement short-term controls for specific CSO impacts, such as solids and floatables, or continued long-term programs such as sewer separation without requiring a formal long-term control plan (LTCP) as envisioned in the Policy. Also, certain States did not assign a very high priority to implementing the CSO Control Policy because of its status as policy rather than regulation.

In December 2000, Congress amended the Clean Water Act to require that any permit, order or decree issued after December 2000, shall conform to the 1994 CSO Control Policy. NPDES permits must require the development and implementation of LTCPs in a timely manner. EPA, through oversight of permits issued to CSO communities, will ensure that permits require development of plans that meet the expectations of the Policy and achieve compliance with the water quality-based and technology-based requirements of the Clean Water Act.

Chapter 3 Conclusion: *There are two main barriers that communities face and need to overcome in reducing CSOs and the water pollution they cause. The most significant is financial – there is presently not enough funding to meet the needs of all CSO communities and many communities are being financially strained. A second major barrier involves finding acceptable locations for CSO facilities, due to such complicating factors as land availability, community opposition, competing land usage, and land ownership.*

EPA Response: EPA recognizes the financial burden that many CSO communities face in developing and implementing CSO control programs. EPA will promote innovative mechanisms, such as the watershed approach, that provide opportunities for communities to phase in the implementation of CSO controls and that allow communities to maximize the use of their limited resources in achieving the greatest environmental benefits.

EPA recognizes that the siting of water pollution control facilities, including CSO facilities, can be problematic. However, many communities have successfully installed control facilities after overcoming local concerns.

EPA Responses to Specific Recommendations

Recommendation 4-1: *EPA develop a system to catalog and disseminate lessons learned and better practices about CSOs. EPA should establish a website where such information can be posted and information easily accessed for use.*

EPA Response: EPA agrees that there is a need to make available to all CSO stakeholders, information and data on CSO control technologies and programs. As a result of the Wet Weather Water Quality Act, EPA is preparing a Report to Congress that is due in December 2003. This report will summarize the extent of the public health and environmental impacts of CSO and sanitary sewer overflows (SSOs), the resources spent by municipalities to address these impacts, and an evaluation of the technologies used by the municipalities to address these impacts. After transmitting this Report to Congress, EPA must maintain a clearinghouse of cost-effective and efficient technologies for addressing the human health and environmental impacts of CSOs and SSOs. This clearinghouse will probably be web-based and will allow CSO stakeholders to benefit from the experiences of other communities that have already initiated programs to control CSOs and SSOs.

Recommendation 5-1: *Amend the CSO Policy to require communities to perform interim reviews of CSO efforts to determine the impact of the project on water quality.*

EPA Response: EPA does not believe that it is necessary to revise the 1994 CSO Control Policy to require communities to perform interim reviews of the impact of CSO control projects on water quality. The appropriate level of monitoring to determine the effectiveness of a specific CSO control project or of an entire long-term CSO control program is highly site-specific. The CSO community and the NPDES permitting authority can negotiate and establish, in an enforceable mechanism, the proper level of monitoring necessary to meet the information and data needs of all stakeholders.

EPA believes the CSO Control Policy and implementing guidance provide appropriate guidelines for the use of monitoring, including interim monitoring where appropriate, in assessing the effectiveness of CSO controls. Under the CSO Policy, communities are expected to develop monitoring plans and perform post-construction compliance monitoring to ensure that water quality standards are being attained. EPA's *Combined Sewer Overflows – Guidance for Monitoring and Modeling* states that in most cases, some monitoring should be conducted during the construction and implementation period to evaluate the effectiveness of CSO controls.

Recommendation 6-1: *Provide a leadership role by working with States and communities to develop watershed approaches that will target priority activities and will ensure that water quality standards are met.*

EPA Response: Currently, EPA is developing a Watershed Permit Framework to further the objectives of its 1994 Watershed Strategy. EPA is developing a plan to promote watershed-based NPDES permits. EPA has held discussions with the Association of State and Interstate Water Pollution Control Administrators and the Association of Metropolitan Sewerage Agencies on this initiative, and will continue to work with these and other interested groups.

The Framework will address the need to provide greater incentives and mechanisms necessary to foster a comprehensive assessment of watershed goals and their current status, the implementation of an agreed-upon watershed monitoring strategy, and the participation and buy-in by all major watershed stakeholders.

Recommendation 6-2: *Provide a leadership role by encouraging States and communities to work with other stakeholders to develop appropriate water quality standards and, when appropriate, revise those standards.*

EPA Response: EPA is committed to facilitating state review of water quality standards and, if appropriate, revising standards to protect the highest attainable designated uses. EPA is working with States and key stakeholders to identify and develop policies and guidance that support appropriate state water quality standards revisions, including the development of sufficient information to justify changes in designated uses, water quality criteria, and implementation methods. These efforts include:

- *Guidance: Coordinating CSO Long-Term Planning With Water Quality Standards Reviews* (EPA-833-R-01-002; July 31, 2001). This guidance describes processes for integrating LTCP development and implementation with water quality standards reviews. EPA's water quality standards regulations provide States with the flexibility to review and revise, as appropriate, the designated uses and water quality standards for surface water bodies. Within the current regulatory framework, States have a number of alternatives for revising water quality standards including the establishment of seasonal uses and the issuance of temporary variances. Revisions lowering the level of protection for the designated use require a Use Attainability Analysis, public participation in the review process, and EPA approval. The *Guidance* uses the current regulatory framework to outline processes for coordination among CSO communities, EPA and State water quality standards program staff and NPDES permitting program staff, the public, and other interested parties. The process can be resource-intensive but, as the *Guidance* concludes, the coordination and cooperation among all parties should ensure that the LTCP, when completed, will prevent CSOs from causing or contributing to the non-attainment of applicable water quality standards. The completed LTCP can also assist the state in determining if the present use is not attainable and in identifying another attainable use.

- *Implementation Guidance for Ambient Water Quality Criteria for Bacteria* (Public Review Draft, May 2002, EPA-823-B-003). When final, this document will provide guidance to States and authorized entities on the adoption and implementation of bacteriological water quality criteria for the protection of waters designated for recreation. In response to comments on the February 2000 draft and subsequent interactions with interested stakeholders, EPA greatly expanded the scope and detail of the guidance. Consequently, additional opportunity for public review is being provided.

- *Draft Strategy for Water Quality Standards and Criteria: Strengthening the Foundation of Programs to Protect and Restore the Nation's Waters* (EPA-823-R-02-001, May 2002). This draft document lays out strategic directions for the water quality standards program over the next seven years in collaboration with other EPA offices and with States and authorized tribes to strengthen and improve the water quality standards and criteria program. The draft strategy is the product of a wide-ranging review of the water quality standards and criteria program within the context of all Clean Water Act programs and the result of more than 50 listening sessions for over 350 people, recommendations from the National Research Council, the General Accounting Office, EPA's Inspector General and EPA's National Environmental Justice Advisory Committee.

- *National Symposium: Designating Attainable Uses for the Nation's Waters*, June 3-4, 2002. EPA hosted this Symposium to hear from interested citizens, governmental officials and regulated parties on the need for additional guidance on establishing the designated uses and the process to follow when making designated uses more or less protective. The proceedings of the Symposium will be available in the Summer of 2002 and will include the invited experts' comments, the 17 presentations, and a summary of the roundtable discussions involving approximately 200 attendees. The Symposium help EPA identify and schedule additional guidance to address key questions on designating and revising designated uses.

- *Tracking Water Quality Standards Reviews on CSO Impacted Waters*. EPA committed to establishing tracking information in the *Guidance: Coordinating CSO Long-Term Planning With Water Quality Standards Reviews* and in the Agency's 2001 Report to Congress. EPA currently is able to identify new or revised standards that the Agency must review and approve or disapprove, and is working with its State partners to obtain additional information to track water quality standards reviews for these waters.

Recommendation 6-3: *Encourage states to adopt water quality standards recognizing seasonal recreational uses.*

EPA Response: States have already adopted seasonal recreational uses where appropriate. EPA's water quality standards regulations at 40 CFR 131.10(f) specifically allow the adoption of seasonal uses as an alternative to reclassifying a water body to uses requiring less stringent criteria. If seasonal uses are adopted, EPA expects states to adjust the water quality criteria to reflect the seasonal uses as long as the criteria do not preclude attainment of the more protective use in another season.

Appendix 2
Distribution

Office of Inspector General

Inspector General (2410)

Headquarters

Assistant Administrator for Water (4101)
Comptroller (2731A)
Agency Audit Followup Coordinator (2724A)
Associate Administrator for Congressional and Intergovernmental Relations (1301A)
Director, Office of Regional Operations (1108A)
Associate Administrator for Communications, Education and Media Relations (1101A)
Director, Office of Wastewater Management (4201)
Director, Permits Division (4203)

Regions

Regional Administrators

CPSIA information can be obtained
at www.ICGtesting.com
Printed in the USA
BVHW061028270921
617616BV00010B/498